Sunset
Patio
Book

By the Editors of Sunset Books
and Sunset Magazine

LANE BOOKS • MENLO PARK, CALIFORNIA

foreword

This completely new edition of the Sunset Patio Book uses the term "patio" in its broadest sense—to include terraces, decks, garden rooms, atriums, and lanais. Concerned with "how-to-plan-it" rather than "how-to-build-it," the book presents an extensive and diversified collection of patio ideas to help the homeowner decide what kind of outdoor room will best suit his needs. It also covers the patio's finishing touches—such as overheads, heating, lighting, and garden pools and fountains.

Over the past several years, hundreds of patios have been scouted by the *Sunset* Editors under the direction of Building Editor Roy Krell. The best of these have been published in *Sunset* Magazine, and most of the ideas presented here were taken from those articles.

Edited by Elizabeth Hogan

Book Design: Susan Lampton

Cover: Sun filters through lath overhead and casts shadows on exposed aggregate patio. Fuchsias in hanging planters and summer annuals in containers add color to intimate patio. Photographed by Ernest Braun at the home of Mr. and Mrs. James Heter, Atherton, California.
Landscape architect: Mary Gordon.

Third Printing May 1972

contents

DECK, house, garden blend as one. Design: Robert Chittock.

Planning Your Patio

By formal definition a patio is the open inner court of a Spanish or Spanish-style house. But by common usage, the term is now applied to almost any form of outdoor sitting or entertaining area. A patio can be a deck, a terrace alongside the house, a separate garden room, a lanai, or an atrium. Whichever kind of patio you decide is right for your particular situation, plan it carefully. If it is to function successfully for you, there are many factors to consider before the construction begins.

THE PATIO IN RELATION TO THE SUN

A south-facing patio is never deserted by the sun. All day, regardless of season or latitude, the sun pours warmth on the outdoor room. However, unless you live in a mild or chilly climate, an overhead structure which will limit di-

CONCRETE PATIO *curves along river rock, lawn. Overhead and screen provide weather protection, plants a touch of color. Design: Warren Rienecker.*

DELIGHTFUL OCTAGONAL PAVILION *has cedar flooring, plywood and sheet metal roof. Coated canvas curtains can be pulled when necessary to shut out sun, wind. Design: Roy Rydell.*

rect sun in the summer is almost essential. Vertical screens, louver panels, or some other kind of side control may also be necessary to block the slanting rays of the sun during the early morning or late afternoon hours. If you live in a hot-climate area and have only a southern location to develop, you may want to add a cooling device such as a vine-laden fence that can be kept moist. During the winter the low sun finds its way under the overhead to warm the patio sufficiently most days. A southern-exposed patio will dry quickly after a rain.

A west-oriented patio can be very hot in the afternoon when it receives the full force of the sun's rays. During the morning the patio is pleasant, but after the sun passes over the roof top, it becomes uncomfortably hot unless sheltered with an overhead. A vertical sun screen may also be needed to block the afternoon sun. In a hot climate, the patio may need some cooling devices such as evaporating water or shrubbery. These patios are not as useful for winter use as southern ones are. During the rainy months, the absence of morning sun keeps the patio damp and cool. However, good surface drainage, a heating unit, and an adjustable overhead will help to make the patio more usable during the winter months.

A patio that faces the east benefits from morning sun and begins to cool off in

WISTERIA trails along roof overhang to add color, shade, and seclusion to small patio off living room. Surface has exposed aggregate finish.

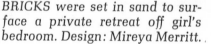

BRICKS were set in sand to surface a private retreat off girl's bedroom. Design: Mireya Merritt.

the afternoon. This orientation is good in a hot climate, and usually needs only a few weather modifiers. Overhead protection is not essential except for shelter from rain or as a means of holding in the heat of the day into the evening. Although an east patio will draw the winter sun until well past the noon hour, it may never quite dry out or warm up enough for winter use. If your climate is cool, you may need supplementary heating, even in the summertime. A fireplace or a radiant heat panel should help.

The coolest site for a patio is a northern exposure. Part of a north-facing patio never receives any direct sun, and if it is in back of a two-story house, the entire patio may pass through the seasons in complete shade. Because of its sheltered position, it does not need an overhead, except as protection from rain. A fiberglass or plastic roof will shed rain but let in the light. Some form of heating is almost essential for real enjoyment of this patio. A north-exposed patio may be most useful if completely enclosed.

Not everyone owns a plot of land that runs true to the four points of the compass, and climate conditions vary across the country. In some situations, wind is more a source of concern than sun; perhaps there is a view to be preserved

MULTI-LEVEL PATIO has roll-around broiler, fireplace, warmer on side of lamp post, room for relaxing, dining. Design: Eriksson & Peters.

INTIMATE breakfast patio is screened from main outdoor area. Design: John Michael Assocs.

and the patio takes a second-choice location. However, the general characteristics of the four patios discussed can be used as a rough guide in working out particular situations.

WHAT SIZE SHOULD YOUR PATIO BE?

Remember that your patio is an outdoor room, not an indoor room, and there is a difference in scale. Do not be afraid to design a large patio—outside, your walls are the trees, your ceiling the sky. Outdoor furniture generally takes up more space than indoor furniture, and you will want to allow room for container plants. Keep in mind the range of activity that will take place on your patio. Ample space is needed for accommodating family and friends and for moving furniture as the weather changes. You might also want room for game tables or for children's wheeled toys.

However, there are sensible limits. An oversized patio can be bleak. No pleasure is derived from a patio that resembles a parking lot or playground. If the size of your lot is so generous that a large patio is necessary to keep everything

BRICK OF PATIO enhances rustic feeling of house and land. Beyond mossy bricks and among mature redwoods is children's play yard, away from but within view of adults' entertaining and relaxing area.

in scale, careful planning can make it manageable by breaking it up into areas that seem comfortable. Squares of plantings inset in paving will break up a monotonous surface; low walls or raised beds can be used to put a stop to a seemingly limitless plane; baffle plantings or fencing can be used to divide the area into two or more functional spaces. The patio can be built on two levels, or the extra space can be devoted to a swimming pool.

If your space is limited, there are several solutions. Reduce the activities planned for the outdoor room in proportion to the space available. A portable barbecue or a unit incorporated into the house chimney would take less space than a freestanding barbecue. Restrained use of plant materials will add charm to the patio—overplanting will add clutter. Use moderate-sized furniture to avoid a crowded feeling.

The small patio can be made to seem larger by various designs. Stepped planting beds lead the eye upward and out of the confined area; tall, vertical screening gives height; a slanting or curved outer boundary or a baffle fence will suggest that there is more patio around the corner. Brick paving, with its small-scale, repetitive patterns, will seem to widen an area; a solid surface

HARMONY is achieved by coordinating house, garden, patio. Lath-sheltered dining patio and living room (above) share same ceiling and end wall (design: Roger Matheson). Decks (top right) blend with surroundings, provide level outdoor living space (design: Fisher-Friedman Assocs.). Paved area (bottom right) connects house and putting green, has pass-through from kitchen, ample seating, pool (design: Tucker & Shields).

will also appear to give more space. Surfacings like tile or flagstone which have emphatic mortar joints will tend to make the patio seem small.

COORDINATE THE PATIO WITH THE HOUSE AND GARDEN

The outdoor room should be firmly integrated with the house. If properly designed and planned, the patio will extend the living area of a house into the outdoors, adding new dimensions to the living room, family room, kitchen, bedroom, or bath. Proximity of the patio to the kitchen facilitates food service— pass-through counters are especially good. Extra chairs or small tables can quickly be moved out-of-doors if the patio is off the living room or family room. A patio near the garage, service yard, or work center allows you to move outdoor furniture, firewood, or plants back and forth with relative ease. A simple wood baffle would easily screen the patio from the work areas.

As in the interior of the house, the traffic pattern through the patio is important. It may be necessary to pass from the house through the patio area to reach sections of the garden. Consider the location of the doors leading into the house

CHERRY TREES shade deck (top left) in corner of yard. Dry stream bed separates sitting area from roofless concrete patio attached to house (design: John Marshall). Garden wall creates privacy for narrow rectangular patio (bottom left) which opens off kitchen, family room (design: Valencia Homes). Sliding glass doors open onto concrete patio (above) surrounded by plantings and shaded by white alder. Wooden steps lead to garden beyond (design: Kathryn Stedman).

and the gate leading into the garden, and if possible provide a pathway around the outside of the patio. Place the barbecue or other cooking facilities, game tables, furniture, and planter boxes out of the line of traffic.

You might want to have a children's patio next to the adults' patio, separated by a fence, gate, or shrubs. This will enable you to watch the children while they are at play, as well as provide additional space for their activities.

If you need more room than the patio affords to entertain large numbers of people, you can make use of an adjacent lawn. A coarse grass will withstand heavy foot traffic for short periods with little or no damage. Another way to accommodate large crowds is by a smaller secondary paved area surfaced with a more informal material. Or, if the patio is separated from the inside by sliding doors, let the guests circulate freely between the indoor and outdoor rooms.

WEATHER MODIFIERS FOR THE PATIO

The number of hours per day your patio is usable depends on the weather. There are several ways to handle the patio that receives too much sun or wind.

CLIMATE can be controlled on the patio. Gas-fed firepit (above) heats volcanic rock, provides warmth on cool days, evenings (design: Warren Lauesen). For coolness and a delightful sound, three openings in brick wall (top right) spill water into decorative pool (design: Jongejan & Garrard). Overhead lath structure (bottom right) provides filtered shade for concrete patio. Spaced 2 by 2's are attached to house rafters, 4 by 4 posts (design: T. W. McAllister & Associates).

Overheads can control both the sun and wind, while glass, fences, screens, or landscaping counteract the wind. Some of the controls are permanent, some adjustable, some removable.

Garden pools can add a cooling touch to your patio, besides being a decorative element and providing a very relaxing sound. To warm your patio, there are outdoor heaters, radiant heating, firepits, or braziers.

ESTIMATE WHAT YOUR PATIO WILL COST

When you are planning your patio, keep in mind approximately how much you want to spend. This could strongly influence your choice of surfacing materials, overhead structures, fences, screens, or plants.

If you design the patio yourself, check prices of materials with local building suppliers, giving them approximate measurements of your patio. If you use a landscape architect or landscape designer, he can tell you what materials are within your price range.

RUNNING BOND PATTERN of bricks (above) set in mortar is durable, easily maintained, and adaptable to a variety of situations. More elaborate is pebble mosaic floor (right) with inset brick pattern —both of the materials are laid in a base of heavy adobe soil (mosaic design: E. Leslie Kiler).

OTHER FACTORS TO CONSIDER

Surfacing materials. Among the wide range of materials to choose from are brick, wood, gravel, flagstone, concrete, or tile. You will want paving that will be pleasant to look at and to walk on. It should be non-skid and non-glare; it should be easy to clean and should dry quickly. Also, the material should blend in with the feeling of the house and the garden. One word of caution—if your patio is to be built around or near a large tree, the root spread may damage the paving, or the paving can damage the tree.

Drainage. The surface of your patio should slope slightly away from the house to allow water to flow off in the proper direction. If you build a level deck, make sure the ground underneath is slightly sloped.

Furniture. Keep in mind the feeling you want your patio to have and furnish it accordingly. There is a wide range of furniture available—from the very casual to the more formal pieces. Consider the portability of the furniture and its resistance to the weather. Built-in benches, especially around the perimeter of the

AZALEA TREES add flourish of color to cozy patio (left). Trailing vines and container plants on ledge break harshness of enclosure wall (design: Lois Brown). Fences, tall plants provide privacy for small area off dining room (above). Surfacing is half concrete, half brick (design: Marc Askew).

patio, are good because they provide permanent and out-of-the-way seating.

Landscaping. Plants on and around your patio offer shade, softening textures, color, and fragrance. Landscaping can also offer protection from the sun and wind as well as provide privacy. Avoid plants which attract bees and other annoying insects, or plants which might present a cleanup problem.

Privacy. Fencing or landscaping can give seclusion to an open patio and at the same time serve as a backdrop for the garden when viewed from inside.

Lighting. Good lighting is both functional and aesthetic. It invites you out-of-doors at night and brings the beauty of the night garden into view from inside the house. Watch the placement of the fixtures, as lights do attract some insects. Low-voltage lighting makes it possible for the homeowner to work with wiring without danger (once past the transformer).

Building regulations. Check your local building codes before your patio plans are finalized. Controls may vary from city to city; however, there are usually regulations when decks, overhangs, electrical work, walls, or structural changes are involved.

BUILT-IN benches enclose brick patio. Design: Roger Osbaldeston.

The Patio as an Extension of a Room

A patio directly off an inside room extends the living area of the house beyond its walls and makes the inside room seem larger and less confining. The patio actually becomes another room of the house, so it is important that the patio, house, and garden be coordinated. Try to convey the feeling of the house in the patio. If your home has a wooded feeling, use a compatible surfacing material and incorporate existing trees into your plan.

A patio can be effective off any room of the house. An outdoor room off the living room or family room is good for general use. It is within easy reach of the entire family and provides level play space for children. It also provides a pleasant view from inside. Sliding glass doors separating the living room from the patio allow for a free flow of traffic when you are entertaining. If you have separate patios off both the living room and the family room, children's activities could be restricted to the latter. Then the patio off the living room could be formally landscaped without chance of plants or containers being bumped by

PATIO is accessible from playroom (left) and from dining room (arched doors with glass panels). Concrete pads, interplanted with grass, allow moisture, oxygen to reach pine tree. Design: Henrik Bull.

BEDROOM OPENS onto patio partly covered by roof overhang. Mexican beach pebbles, planting bed decorate outdoor room. Design: John Averill.

wheeled toys. A kitchen patio can be small and intimate, or if the kitchen opens to the back yard it can be the main patio. A pass-through counter is especially convenient in this type of situation and facilitates serving. Bedroom and bathroom patios can give a garden view to the rooms they adjoin. These patios are usually private and are enclosed by a wall or fence. Patios can also give dimension to rooms that are generally small.

A room can have a private patio of its own, or more than one room can open onto the same patio. A patio can run the length or width of a house, even curving around corners and fitting the contours of the house. Sometimes the situation calls for separate patios—one on the shady side and one on the sunny side of the house. You may want a large patio for all to use, and a separate one that is more private. When deciding on where your patio (or patios) will be, consider which room (or rooms) would benefit most from the patio. Also consider the lot —where it is most possible to put a patio. If a level patio adjoining the house is impossible, you can design a multilevel patio. Or, if the lot slopes steeply, the terrace can be landscaped to provide some level space for outdoor entertaining and relaxing.

Outdoor living with connecting patios

Both major living areas of this house, the living-dining room and kitchen-family room, open directly to brick patios linked together by a walkway of bricks and railroad ties. The railroad ties retain the soil where there is a grade change and also function as steps.

Design: Ralph Edwards.

TWO PATIOS are connected by steps of railroad ties, separated by cluster of native oaks.

DECKING (at right) is walkway from living room, matches built-in bench. Railroad ties frame patio.

BUFF-COLORED BRICKS contrast with railroad ties darkened with creosote. Larger patio is just a few steps off the kitchen.

Breezeway patio—ideal in a hot climate

Situated between the living areas of the house and the carport, the breezeway patio makes a pleasant outdoor room. The spaced-lath overhead gives the brick-paved patio filtered shade but doesn't interfere with air circulation. The patio is completely shaded by the house until midmorning and by the carport roof from midafternoon to evening. A 5-foot wall on the south side keeps out what sun the overhead doesn't catch.

On the north side of the breezeway is a rear terrace, open to the sky, which extends the usable outdoor living space.

Design: Gordon Maas Luepke.

LIVING ROOM, KITCHEN open onto breezeway patio protected from sun by house, carport roof.

Patio in the middle of a two-pavilion house

A glass-walled hallway connects the two pavilions which make up this burnt adobe house. One pavilion houses the living and entertaining areas, the other the sleeping areas.

Between the two pavilions and bordering one side of the glass hallway is a small brick (basket-weave design) patio. The living room opens onto the patio as does the kitchen, which has a pass-through counter that facilitates outdoor serving.

Design: Bennie M. Gonzales.

SHADED and protected from wind, patio is ideal for dining.

Living room, family room form L around patio

When this house was remodeled and enlarged, a patio was included to fit the L-shaped structure. The new wing of the house, consisting of a family room, laundry room, and half bath, opens onto the patio through sliding glass doors. A very small deck off the family room steps down to the patio. The living room also opens onto the patio through French doors. The brick surface, mortared in a basketweave pattern, is easy to maintain.

Design: Rosekrans & Broder.

LARGE OUTDOOR ROOM provides more living, entertaining space by extending family room (left) and living room (through French doors). Patio is open to the sky but is shaded by trees, house structure.

Brick terraces off
the dining areas

BRICK TERRACE (left), off dining room, was raised to floor level to make indoor-outdoor access easier (design: Burr Richards). Patio above has plant groupings to soften square shape; benches have brick base (design: Robert Ferris).

House addition
adds a patio

SHADED by house and eucalyptus (at left), patio opens from family room through sliding door. Surface is sections of bricks separated by header boards. Plants soften stucco wall. Design: Jones & Peterson.

These patios serve both living, dining rooms

OLD BRICKS dividing 3-foot squares of paving relate small, intimate patio to house. Egg-crate overhead has clear plastic panels for rain protection. Supporting roof posts were placed so that view through glass-paned doors would not be blocked. Design: Roberta Wightman.

TWO-LEVEL PATIO has brick and concrete block wall for divider. Larger area off dining room is paved; lower one off living room is part paving, part lawn. Design: Rosalind Wheeler.

Split-level patio is complete outdoor room

A paved patio on two levels opened up a small porch that was too small and shady and had thick shrubbery which threatened a view of sunsets.

One portion of the remodeled patio is at the house floor level, another is three steps lower at the lawn grade. The steps also provide extra seating for large outdoor gatherings.

The low brick wall around the patio, although usually used for plant display, can easily be cleared and used as a bench. Cushions kept handy make seating more comfortable.

An open firepit with raised coping of brick serves as a fireplace. It is lined with firebrick and also has a drain installed under six inches of gravel to carry off surplus water in winter. When roasting hot dogs over the coals, you can sit on the brick coping around the firepit.

Design: John C. Lindahl.

BEFORE REMODEL paved area under roof overhang was too small. Plants were overgrown.

LIVING ROOM opens onto two-level patio with an exposed aggregate finish. Low brick walls partly frame new sitting area, display container plants. Mature tree provides some shade.

WIDE STEPS connect upper and lower levels, also provide extra seating close to firepit.

Kitchen wall was opened to add a patio

OUTDOOR ROOM was added to update exterior of house and to increase living space. Patio begins at floor level of kitchen, then steps down to lawn. Sliding glass doors replaced small back window; back door remains, is screened by podocarpus in containers. Lath overhead provides filtered shade. Design: Armstrong & Sharfman.

Spanish-style patio off the kitchen

LATH and leafy grape vines shade and cool patio's dining and sitting areas. Tiled bench and table are just outside kitchen window and adjacent to kitchen door. Tile paving is same as used inside. Design: Peter Edwards.

These patios are shaped in geometric forms

FOCAL POINT of patio is podocarpus stretching tall between house and patio overhead. Cut slate is durable surface. Design: C. Jacques Hahn.

PEBBLE-PAVED patio blends with pebble-mulched garden beds. Table umbrella shades diners as patio is exposed to full sun. Design: Thomas Nishimura.

CONCRETE PATIO is spacious enough for numerous activities. Sandbox adjoins patio, has drain tiles to carry water away. Raised concrete firepit placed in angle of built-in bench is used as base for barbecue. Design: Gene Zema.

Patios bring together house and garden

PAVED TERRACE is off family room, kitchen. Heating coils under floor warm patio; house eaves provide shelter. Design: Robert Chittock.

TUBS of golden bamboo, ground cover around patio edge, ivy on fence make dramatic backdrop for outdoor room when viewed from inside.

OAK-SHADED brick patio was raised to floor level of dining room, furnished with container plants. Design: Edwards-Pitman.

Changing levels, surfacing give dimension

SMALL CITY PATIO is part deck, part used brick set in sand. Container plants make up for lack of planting space. Design: Herbert Kosovitz.

FAMILY ROOM opens onto concrete patio. Overhead shades seating area. Design: George Fuller.

TERRACE off living room, bedroom is paved in exposed aggregate and brick, has built-in seating. Beyond spacious terrace is garden. Design: Robert Chittock.

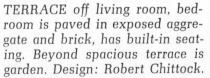

A terraced private garden

Before this small garden was remodeled, two serious drawbacks had to be overcome. The lot sloped up steeply 30 feet behind the house, and poor drainage due to seepage from the slope kept the ground soggy during much of the year. Also, the entrances from the house into the garden were inconvenient.

An airy skylighted garden room, which enlarges the house, now joins the garden and the living room in an easy transition. To solve the drainage problem, sections of perforated plastic drainage pipe were buried in a gravel-filled trench at the base of the slope to catch excess water from the bank. A freeform brick terrace, a continuation of the brick flooring used in the new garden room, extends into the garden.

Design: W. David Poot.

LOW, BROAD brick steps begin at terrace level, lead up to a sunning area at top of bank.

GARDEN ROOM opens onto freeform brick terrace. Shades can be pulled for sun control.

SLOPE AND HEDGE at one side of garden room provide privacy; container plants add color.

Sitting areas march up the slope

A three-level garden was carved from a slope so steep that nine truckloads of soil were hauled away to shape a series of planes climbing to a sun deck platform.

To keep maintenance to a minimum, large areas of paving were used. From the top level, such expanses of concrete might look harsh, but from the lower patio level, they are foreshortened and unobtrusive. "Needle Point" ivy, a fine-textured ground cover, helps hold the sculptured slopes. A small dichondra lawn occupies part of the lower patio space.

Design: Eriksson, Peters & Thoms.

LIVING ROOM has this view of terraced garden. Paving, ground cover make for low maintenance.

LOWEST TERRACE is reached from living room, bedroom. Paved patio offers sun or filtered shade.

DECK provides generous space for outdoor entertaining, is also a good place for sunbathing.

You step down to these patios

ROOFED PORCH (above) adjoining house steps down to two-level paved patio (design: Roberta Wightman). Patio at right has broad steps leading up to engawa, protected by overhang, at floor level of house (design: Thorne of Berkeley).

AIRY LATH ROOF of 1 by 2 strips spaced an inch apart casts shade over patio for comfortable outdoor living. Steps go from living room to spacious two-level brick patio. Design: Mildred Davis.

A veranda wrapped in glass

TRANSLUCENT AND CLEAR glass panels enclose three sides of veranda, while floor-to-ceiling windows separate garden room from living room. Overhead, brick flooring, seating make area very livable. Design: Williams & Williams.

Loggia for relaxing, gardening

ROOF OVERHANG supported by posts provides shade and a cool place for outdoor sitting, also protects plants from winter frosts. Bricks cemented together on their sides form floor of portico as well as semi-circular planting beds.

Private patios
off the bedrooms

BEDROOM FLOOR continues out to brick-paved terrace on same level, through wide roll-away glass wall. Design: Cliff May.

SMALL OUTDOOR ROOM, one step below bedroom level, is reached through sliding glass door. Rectangular space is partly paved with pads of exposed aggregate; perimeter, end areas are landscaped for soft garden effect. Fence of ripped mahogany ensures privacy. Design: Robert Chittock.

INTIMATE PATIO has paved area for sitting. Round pads across lawn lead to low ledge used for display of container plants. Note how patio roof extends into bedroom to keep morning sun out. Design: Eriksson, Peters & Thoms.

TUCKED INTO HILLSIDE, bedroom opens to private patio, partly shaded by roof overhang. Stone wall curves around hill, passes through bedroom. Flagstone paving harmonizes with feeling of wall. Design: Calvin Straub & Denis Kutch.

Intimate patio off the bath

SMALL ENCLOSED GARDEN gives bathroom feeling of outdoor room. Tropical plants thrive in protected surrounding, border terrazzo paving. Fencing is translucent fiberglass panels. Design: L. K. Smith.

POOL with fountain of clay "leaves" is focal point of entry.

The Entry Patio

Most patios are located in back of the house, since this is the area that usually offers the most space, privacy, and seclusion from the activities of the street, and close proximity to the kitchen, dining room, and garden. However, if the back yard already has a patio and you want additional outdoor living space, or if the garden takes up the entire back yard, an entry patio may be your answer. Many livable outdoor rooms are placed in front, between the house and the street. And this may be one way to get the most out of the front garden.

An entry patio makes a hospitable entrance; however, as it does not always give full privacy, careful planning is necessary. Usually the area available is limited, and local setback ordinances have to be considered. You may want to screen the entry patio from the street, but you may not want to completely hide the house. Check with your local building inspector concerning height limits for fences in front. When constructing a fence or planting shrubbery, coordinate it as much as possible with your house, garden, and neighborhood.

ENTRY DECK has built-in bench for seating. Redwood rounds, Japanese maple, ferns at base of tree give woodsy effect. Design: Theodore Milhous.

KITCHEN COUNTER extends into garden room as eating, serving counter. High masonry walls provide privacy; open to sky, entry is light, airy. Design: Donald Blair, Jack Buktanica.

TWO WOOD SCREENS partly enclose paved entry, offer some privacy for street-facing windows, patio. Lot slopes to front, side; steps make pleasant grade transition. Design: John Herbst, Jr., & Assocs.

A cool and private entry patio

THREE GIANT circular steppingstones lead to sunken paved patio, a place to sit or entertain. Stones act as bridge over pool; fountain brings cooling touch to entry. Design: Kenneth K. Hayashi.

ENTRY is hidden from street by high, curving brick wall. Landscaping around the enclosure and plants in raised beds soften harshness of wall. Overhead provides some shade to patio entrance.

It's an entry, a patio, and a garden room

This enclosed area has an unusually attractive and functional indoor-outdoor relationship. Located between the family room and bedroom wing with the living-dining area in the rear, it serves both as an entry court and outdoor living room.

An expanded metal screen, added for aesthetic reasons, not for privacy, softens and adds a filagreelike design to the translucent glass wall of a hallway along the bedroom wing. The long horizontal lines of the screen, slightly curved to match a bench in front, increase the patio's apparent size and add feeling to the somewhat harsh rectangle.

To filter the sun in the space open to the sky, a tree (an evergreen pear) was used instead of an architectural feature. The tree's greenness, texture, and varying shadow patterns offer a pleasant contrast to the rigidity of four walls, paving, and other structural elements. Star jasmine grows at the base of the tree.

The raised bed and planted corners help to break up the large paved surface. A climbing fern asparagus makes a filmy tracery against the screen.

Design: Mary Gordon, Anshen & Allen.

CLOSE RELATIONSHIP to living room, family room, bedrooms, makes entry patio handy place for relaxing and entertaining. Diamond pattern of metal screen is picked up in large expanse of pavement.

Outrigger walls shelter patio

Two-story-high outrigger walls that stand 10 feet out from the glass-walled house shelter this street-facing patio. Appearing from the front to be free-standing, the walls are actually supported by extensions of the house walls at the ends and by horizontal metal braces. One section has a giant arch, the other a series of glassless windows and doors. Between them and the house is a sheltered outdoor sitting area and container garden.

The walls also provide the house with a degree of privacy from the street and cut sky glare without interfering with a view. In the winter, when the sun is to the south, they bounce daylight back into the house. Because it is located in the desert, this house is oriented to the north so the protective wall sections never get the full impact of the sun.

Design: James A. Gresham.

WALLS with glassless windows, doors create an open-to-the-sky patio—an extension of the house.

ARCHWAY frames entrance to patio, house. Sliding glass doors in back of table open to inside.

PARKING AREA is hidden from patio view, garden by low wall.

This front yard is a brick-paved patio

BETWEEN HOUSE and ivy-covered wall is brick-paved entry garden. Patio receives full sun; low deck across front of house is shaded by trellis. Design: The Bumgardner Partnership.

Streetside deck is outdoor room

BRICK STEPS lead from driveway to front door (far left of photograph). Deck above garage goes around two sides of living room, extending usable living space of entryway. Design: Raymond Kappe.

Through the baffle is a private retreat

This front garden shows a trim, dignified face to passers-by and a much different face to anyone in the private area on the other side of the brick wall. The streetside garden is a neat, clean combination of ground cover, low hedge, brick wall, and ivy wall rimmer. It requires little watering and always looks groomed because the plants are easy to care for.

Around a baffle in the brick wall, the inside garden is an almost constantly colorful scene of camellias, carnations, daphne, hydrangeas, and iris. There is a patio off the front door for outdoor eating, relaxing, and entertaining.

Design: George E. Martin.

ENTRY PATIO is hidden from street by brick wall. You pass through baffle to enter garden.

Spacious but secluded front court

SIX-FOOT-HIGH fence, dense shrubs make entry court private. Paving of squares and rectangles has interesting grid pattern of texture—some sections are smooth, some are seeded with pebbles. Design: Richard Beeson.

Three houses share an entryway

Originally there were three separate gardens in front of three separate houses, each on a 25-foot-wide lot. Relandscaping connected the three gardens, yet preserved their individual character and privacy.

You approach the three houses from the street along the straight, narrow walk (see photo below). To the left of the walk is a sheltered, private patio (bottom right photo). Ahead of the patio is a wide central deck (top right photo), the main unifying element of the design. All three houses are reached via the central deck.

Design: Dan Rolfs.

DECK is at end of entry path. Steps lead ahead to upper patio or sharp right to house entrance.

IRON GATE opens to narrow walk which leads to houses. Pittosporum shades ivy ground cover.

GRAVEL-PAVED patio separates entry path from garden next door. Landscaping, fencing make outdoor room private.

A patio between the carport, family room

HOUSE, FRONT GARDEN were remodeled after walnut tree (photo above) died. Garage was converted to multipurpose room; carport was added. Right photo shows paved and lath-sheltered entry garden through former garage door.

FLAT-ROOFED CARPORT at left and remodeled garage at right form two sides of new paved entry behind fence. Part of carport's roof extends over patio and provides shade. Design: L. K. Smith.

Central patio inside front gate

HIGH FENCE makes street-facing court private. Patio is bordered by the three wings of house. Paving is loose-laid brick. Design: The Bumgardner Partnership; David Poot.

Privacy beside the front door

This streetside patio was designed to ensure privacy on a busy residential street. The 600-square-foot garden includes an exposed aggregate patio surrounded by plantings of bamboo, mugho pine, azaleas, and other shrubs. All this is hidden from front view; only the front walk and entry are visible from the street.

The fence is made of 1 by 1's, spaced ½ inch apart on both sides of 2 by 4-inch stringers. The ½-inch gaps allow air circulation—important, since the garden is on the warm south side.

Design: Gil Rovianek.

ATTRACTIVE fence screens large entry garden from street. Planting square holds mugho pine, sedum; bamboo is at back.

Courtyard in the Spanish tradition

PATIO extends space of living room—its natural adobe walls repeat inside wall surface.

ARCHED DOOR serves as main entry from driveway. House on three sides opens directly onto patio.

TILED FOUNTAIN is focal point of courtyard. Corner areas are planted with shrubs, leaving large usable brick-paved area for outdoor living. Design: Dick McNeil.

An interior courtyard beyond an entry court

SHUTTERED DOORS open from graveled entry to courtyard. Across patio, sliding glass door opens to living room (above). Patio has ample room for setting up tables and chairs for entertaining (right).

ROOF OVERHANG provides cool, shaded buffer zone for rooms along patio and for plants. Paving is irregular rectangular blocks bounded by dichondra. Design: C. Jacques Hahn, J. Charles Hoffman.

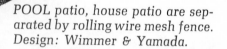

POOL patio, house patio are separated by rolling wire mesh fence. Design: Wimmer & Yamada.

The Patio around the Pool

A poolside patio creates a frame for the swimming pool and provides a safe walkway for swimmers, a necessary drainage surface, and an outdoor entertaining area. If possible, the patio should be spacious, as poolside furniture and sunbathers take up a surprising amount of room. There should always be enough room for non-swimmers to relax without threat of being splashed.

The patio and pool should complement each other. If the surface of the patio is extended right to the water's edge, the smooth, uninterrupted poolside surface draws the eye to the water, integrating the pool and the garden. Choose a patio surface that will blend with the feeling of the pool. A brushed or textured concrete or a pebbled surface have colors that complement water, tile, and coping. Warm earth colors enhance the blue tint of the water and seem natural in a garden. Wood decking, often the only usable material on a hillside lot, is effective as a raised sunning deck or as an architectural extension of a concrete area. Bricks, with their pleasing form and texture, can be used in either large

AROUND SWIMMING POOL is spacious tiled patio available to townhouse dwellers for recreational use. Design: Hall & Goodhue for Burchfiel Meadows.

BRIDGE across pool is unifying element between house and deck. Design: John H. Ostwald.

quantities or just to soften expanses of concrete. If your patio surface becomes slippery when wet, treat it with a solution of aluminum oxide mixed with waterproof paint or a clear compound.

Plan the landscaping around the pool carefully. Wide decked areas or raised beds will protect plants which are easily damaged by chlorine. Container plants bring color close to the pool and can be moved out of reach of splashing water when the pool has heavy use. The expanse of water in the pool produces high humidity, especially if the pool is heated, so plants susceptible to mildew are likely to be affected. Use only those whose foliage will withstand moisture. For low maintenance select trees and shrubs that drop a minimum of leaves, fruit, resin, and other debris. Avoid those that attract bees.

Provide some shaded areas for sitting around the pool. Pipe inserts in the patio allow umbrellas to be arranged for sun control and color accents. Fencing, house wings, or a simple roof can also give shade.

A two-way counter between kitchen and patio is helpful for poolside dining. It permits indoor serving and outdoor eating so that wet swimmers do not have to pass through the house. Place the dining table far enough from the pool so diners do not get splashed and so debris does not fall into the pool.

Octagonal deck frames circular pool

An octagonal wooden deck, surrounding a 32-foot-diameter swimming pool, repeats the contours of the nearby pavilion and provides seating and lounging space. Behind the swimming pool, the deck widens to accommodate built-in benches on the perimeter; pool equipment occupies space under this section of the deck.

The surrounding garden, almost classic in its simplicity, has strong, clean lines and minimal, all-green, basic plantings that do not compete with the natural setting. Container plants such as geraniums offer bright splashes of color on the deck and living room terrace.

Design: Roy Rydell.

COBBLESTONE stepping pads set in concrete, juniper beds link house, pavilion, and pool.

OCTAGONAL PAVILION opens onto cedar boardwalk leading to deck, garden, circular pool.

TERRACE of exposed aggregate off living room adjoins pool deck.

Poolside living in a limited space

A fresh and innovative solution turned a very confined area between the house and a retaining wall into a swimming pool and lounging area. The pool was wrapped around a corner of the house, with an exposed aggregate wall forming the limits of two sides of the pool to provide sitting space and diving platforms.

Since there was little decking, a main outdoor gathering, entertaining, and sunning area was built —a five-sided platform, partly enclosed by a low wall, complete with lounging pads, small corner tables, and a gas-fed firepit. The platform's sloping walls serve as a backrest, and on warm days they soak up the sun's heat and then radiate it back in the evening. A round table can be set up at the side or directly over the firepit when no fire is needed. Only 12 inches high, it works well for outdoor buffets and for sit-down meals.

Design: Donald Brinkerhoff & Associates.

Table design: Larry B. Seewack.

POOL WALL is exposed aggregate, as is five-sided platform beyond pool, next to house.

TABLE has plastic laminate top, edges, is set over firepit. Smaller tables fit into corners between pads.

SUNNING, entertaining area has firepit for cool days, nights.

Angular patios complement this pool

The shape of the pool and the adjacent paving provides the same strong shadow patterns found in the surrounding desert. From the house or poolside you look out across a sheet of water that appears to flow into the desert. The illusion is achieved by eliminating the coping at one end of the pool and bringing the water level up flush with the side. Across the pool from the house is a raised sitting area, partly shaded by palms and cactus, for entertaining or sunbathing.

Design: Guy Greene.

SMALL PATIO surrounds pond of aquatic plants (above). Raised sitting area (right) is across swimming pool from house, gets afternoon shade.

WALKWAY around swimming pool has thick-pebbled surface; patios have exposed aggregate finish. Water that splashes out of pool flows over concrete apron away from pool, sinks into desert sand.

Pool, patio, and deck on a small, steep lot

A small paved patio and an expanse of lawn were remodeled to include a new patio, a pool, and a deck. The pool was squeezed into an area bounded by the house and drive on three sides and by a steep bank on the other. In fact, one corner of the pool is partly freestanding, and the deck around that corner is built out over the bank.

When the pool was added, the garden was relandscaped. A wall between the parking area and the pool was added for safety and privacy. Trees were planted to shade a dining area near the pool. A wood deck was built out over the canyon to create additional level space. The pool heater, filter, and pump are located under the deck.

Design: Joseph Cobb, Jr.

PATIO, shaded by Brazilian pepper trees, has dappled paving made by pressing smooth black pebbles into white mortar. Wood deck is best place for afternoon sunning. At left, over low wall, is lily pond.

A patio and play area around the pool

RAISED FIREPIT (right) is for heating patio or outdoor cooking. Under balcony is play area (above). Deck at left is bridge across to pool patio. Design: Sid Galper & Assocs., Don Alfredo Tomas.

Brick wall frames pool and patio

BURNT ADOBE WALL extends from house to enclose outdoor living area. House is positioned so that living room, dining room, and bedrooms look out onto patio and pool. Design: J. R. Schibbley.

Three decks
for poolside living

REAR AREA of garden sloped, so pool was set against bank. Deck in foreground is built over bank that slants to terrace at house floor level.

DECKED AREA around circular swimming pool is large enough for poolside recreation. Pool is prefabricated, above-the-ground model.

RAISED DECK provides sunbathing, seating, eating, recreation area near pool but out of range of water splashed by swimmers. Design: Armand Ramirez.

Three simple but effective pool patios

GEOMETRIC ANGLES make interesting pattern in paving of patio around pool. Beyond shallow end stairs climb toward house, dining terrace.

EXPOSED AGGREGATE patio around pool has food-serving facilities (sink, small refrigerator) for entertaining. House, several steps up from patio, overlooks pool. Design: Richard B. Nelson.

POOL has two patio areas—an angled deck attached to house and a small patio on garden side.

From house to patio to swimming pool

SIMPLE CONCRETE PATIO (left), brightened with container plants, ground cover along walkway, is good sunning area next to pool (design: Waldo Scott, Duane Spurling, Robert F. Brown). Patio above also has simple surfacing, but design of pool and of house gives more formal feeling (design: George W. Christiansen).

GLASS-WALLED WALKWAYS connect house pavilions and, through sliding glass doors, open onto pool and patio area. Pool lines are simple; plants add color to patio. Design: Fisher-Friedman Assocs.

HILLSIDE deck creates level space for outdoor living. Design: Campbell-Michael-Yost.

Low-Level and Hillside Decks

Decks are patios with a wood surfacing. They first became popular with hillside homeowners who wanted level outdoor living space—a place to sit and enjoy the view. Decks were more practical and less expensive to build than paved patios because the decks were supported by piers, eliminating the need for extensive grading and filling. Today, low-level decks are gaining in popularity. In this situation, decking materials may be more expensive than paving; however, little or no grading is required.

Decks are very versatile—they can be designed to fit an informal or formal situation. Maintenance requirements are minimal. Wood is a quick-drying surface and is springier than concrete or brick.

When planning a deck, especially if you live on a hillside, it is best to consult with a landscape architect, contractor, or engineer. He can advise you on such matters as drainage, soil retention, grading, connecting the house to the deck, vertical supports, and the spanning distance for various sizes of lumber.

MAIN LIVING AREAS of house shelter deck. Glass wall thwarts wind but not view. Roofed-over strip provides rain protection. Design: Fletcher & Finch.

POSITIONING of surface, angular built-in seating add dimension to simple lines of house.

LIVING ROOM is bordered by decking, has expansive view of hillside surroundings. Two sides of deck are roofed, provide shade for outdoor sitting, keep the inside cool. Design: Francis Leighton.

This deck wraps around the house

This deck, level with the interior floor and in an L shape around the northwest corner of the house, is really three decks in one. The largest area, at the corner, has built-in benches and space enough to accommodate a large group. It is partly shaded in summer by a purple-leaf plum tree. Joining this space is a somewhat more secluded area with table and chairs, along the north wall of the dining room. The third section is a balcony that continues the deck line across the west face of the house, where the lot slopes off more steeply.

The west wall is partially shaded from the afternoon sun by a roof overhang and an extension of 2 by 6's, spaced and set on edge. Roll-down wood slat blinds are used when the sun sinks low in the late afternoon.

Peeled log poles used for vertical posts, deck rail, and bench backs add a rustic effect, augmented by the natural finish of the deck and the flat stones used as steps off the deck.

Design: Burr Richards.

REDWOOD 2 by 4's in 4-foot squares form deck. House wall shades dining section.

BUILT-IN BENCH (left) has protective rail; deck is four steps above ground. Corridor extension (above) has access to dining room's sliding doors. Deck added 480 square feet of level space to house.

Three floor-level decks
for outdoor living

SMALL, SIMPLE DECK off living room captures feeling of house, is partially shaded by mature Douglas fir. Design: Harris, Reed, & Litzenberger.

GLASS DOORS in kitchen open to fenced-in, floor-level deck. Design: William Hocking.

TRELLIS overhead shelters spacious deck. Both bedroom and living room open onto outdoor room. Design: Witold T. Willer.

Low-level deck creates new garden space

FLOOR-LEVEL deck, 24 feet wide, is reached through kitchen door. Deck has built-in seating; evergreen pear tree grows through well. Fence screens drive. Design: Armstrong & Sharfman.

A redwood deck from old church pews

RAISED DECK made of lumber from old church pews spans width of yard, provides dry surface where lawn used to be. Deck is several steps up from concrete patio that adjoins house. Design: Roy Boyles.

This house has decks both front and back

The front deck of this house was so pleasant that the uninteresting rear garden was converted into a second deck. The new outdoor room, designed to match the character of the house and to take only a minimum of maintenance, opened up the living room and dining room. The rectangle-shaped deck steps down into the garden.

Design: John Michael Associates.

REAR DECK extends living room outdoors. Overhead beams, pairs of 2 by 8's on edge, let sun in but give some screening from neighboring houses.

STREETSIDE DECK off master bedroom is fenced for privacy, has sunning platform-bench.

CORNER of new deck is like a room, with enclosure on three sides, Mexican furniture, wrought iron candelabrum overhead, hanging pots of asparagus ferns.

Ground-level deck replaced a gravel patio

A new deck added freshness and excitement to this small private garden. Formerly a graveled sitting area, the garden was remodeled without disturbing the plants which had matured to give shade and seclusion.

The deck area was opened to the upper portion of the garden by cutting through a hedge and adding some steps. The decking is stained heart redwood 2 by 6's with a 2 by 4 set every 3 feet to break the pattern.

Design: Roy Rydell.

CONTAINER PLANTS add color, shrubbery and fencing a feeling of intimacy to patio. Deck is reached through sliding glass doors of house. Steps lead up to gravel area, garden, and street.

This deck sits on top a carport

The exterior of this hillside house was updated with the addition of a new entrance court and a double carport with a decked-over top. The sun deck on top of the carport greatly increased the livability of the house by adding 400 square feet of level, usable, outdoor space.

Design: William J. Bain, Jr.

DOUBLE CARPORT supports deck screened from street by a 6 foot 8 inch fence of 1 by 1-inch cedar (above). Kitchen doors (left) open onto deck; folding screen hides work area.

TUBS OF PINES, Douglas fir beyond deck, wood surface, water in background give outdoor room a cool feeling. Built-in seating has protective rail. Barbecue can be moved for best positioning.

One deck faces the ocean, the other the mountains

Sitting on a sand dune, this beach house is almost completely surrounded by decks which extend living space to the front and the rear. The house is L-shaped, with the living room opening onto both the ocean-view and mountain-view decks.

On the ocean side, the deck is glassed-in at one end for wind protection. A roof overhang gives a feeling of cover, without cutting out the sun or light on dark days. The deck on the mountain side is protected from the sun by an extension of the house roof and from the cooling ocean breezes by the house itself.

Design: Lutah Maria Riggs & Richard B. Nelson.

DINING ROOM and living room have sliding glass doors which open to ocean-facing deck.

GLASSED-IN end of deck makes sunny, wind-protected pocket. Roof members extend out to give feeling of cover without cutting out sun and view.

LIVING ROOM looks out on streetside deck, has view of mountains. Roof protects deck from the sun; house shelters it from the ocean breezes.

Central deck
for a narrow beach lot

All living areas of this beach house open to a large deck (23 by 34 feet). The house is oriented toward the water—only the front door and two pairs of narrow windows face the road. When you enter the front door, you're in a covered hallway that leads to the deck between two bunk rooms on the left and the major enclosed living areas of the house on the right.

Design: Bittman & Sanders.

ENTRY (at left) is through covered hallway that leads to deck. Bunk rooms open onto deck, as do the bath, the kitchen, and the living room.

GLASS WALLS separate living room from deck. Roof extension is sun shade for inside room, deck.

LARGE DECK can handle a crowd. Roof beams (4 by 18-inch between 3 by 8 verticals) extend angled house roof over deck.

Three decks aimed for an ocean view

BEACH DECKS are slightly elevated but at floor level of houses. Roof overhangs provide some weather protection. Design: Liddle & Jones (above); May & McElhinney (right).

ROOFED DECK runs along side of house facing beach. Den, living room, and bedroom open onto deck. Driftwood, logs, stones hide supporting posts. Design: Kirk, Wallace, McKinley A.I.A. & Assocs.

Decks for steep shoreline lots

SUN DECKS of twin houses extend out over water, have platform for lounging. Broad steps between houses lead down to lake. Side decks provide additional outdoor room. Design: Howard Kinney.

DECK with built-in seating and protective rail gives outdoor living space to house perched on boulder-strewn site. On upper level, front bedrooms open to sheltered balcony. Design: Campbell & Hoover.

This garden steps down to the beach

An interrupted stairway with flat outdoor areas for sitting and entertaining turned a steep hillside lot into an attractive and usable garden. It also made the beach easily accessible from the house.

On a level below the main living areas of the house, there is a combination concrete terrace and wood deck (the concrete is on grade and the deck is built out over the hillside). This is the main outdoor living area, with built-in benches and a colorful array of container plants. From here you descend in two easy stages to a flat lawn area, and then by another stairway to the beach.

Design: Richard Beeson.

HEXAGONAL SHAPE is repeated in bench, landings, steppingstones (above). Beach is below retaining wall, built to create level area for lawn, then backfilled with soil to support turf.

Floor-level deck for a sloping lot

LIVING ROOM, four steps lower than rest of house, opens onto its own deck. Beyond living room, deck continues around house on higher level. Design: Robert Price.

A grand deck
for a wooded ridgetop

A 2,000-square-foot deck provides generous outdoor space for this house on a wooded ridgetop, adds visual depth to the view-facing rooms, and contributes privacy by blocking the view of the house from the road below. As the deck is so spacious, shrubs planted in the deck slots act as space dividers to relate areas of the deck to the bedroom, living room, and kitchen.

The deck, which runs the length of the house, has a raised belvedere for seating. Around one side of the house, the deck becomes a bridge that leads to a platform and a children's play yard.

Design: Richard W. Painter.

ELEVATED AREA at edge of deck has seating space, high railing for safety, trellis overhead.

BRIDGE WALKWAY leads from deck to play area, has wall and overhead of spaced boards.

PLATFORM, adjacent to children's play yard, has protective railings, is good lookout point.

Three decks, an engawa expand this house

This hillside home was expanded without having to enlarge the rooms. It was done by adding three decks and an engawa, plus balconies off bedrooms and the study.

The smallest deck is off the living room and is used for dining and entertaining. Two decks step down the slope below it. A 4-foot-wide engawa runs the full width of the house at the playroom floor level, three steps above the largest deck. Beyond and 5 feet lower is a smaller deck with a swing, climbing tower, and sandbox, reached by stairs behind a grape arbor.

Design: Robert Chittock.

GRAPE VINE is trained over trellis for shade and foliage for largest deck. Beyond arbor, steps lead down to a deck with play equipment.

SMALLEST DECK, at living room level, has protective rails, is covered with carpeting. Pots of pines, pelargoniums, marguerites, decorate upper deck, which overlooks large deck off the playroom.

CHILDREN'S deck is outdoor extension of lower-level playroom. Balconies are off bedrooms.

The stair landing became a deck

The living room and kitchen are at the rear of this split-level house, a full story above the garden. Getting to usable outdoor space used to require going downstairs.

The small stair landing was turned into a 12 by 14-foot deck. It increased the outdoor living space and extends the indoor rooms opening off it. Siding to match the house encloses the deck and sheathes the new stairway.

Design: Ridenour & Cochran.

BEFORE REMODELING, stairway was open. Landing was too small for effective outdoor use.

NEW DECK cantilevers from second floor over patio. Stairway, deck were sheathed to match house.

LANDING was turned into deck made of ⅝-inch exterior plywood over 2 by 10's, is carpeted.

Deck complex includes garden and waterfalls

Perched on a steep hillside, this house has a deck complex designed to provide outdoor living areas for adults and play space for children.

Full of surprises, the deck has the effect of a hanging garden with bamboo, pine, and fatsia growing through the center. Waterfalls spill from pool to pool. A vine maple grows in a large concrete container. Paving surrounds a circular scrap of lawn. The sod was laid over porous gravel behind the concrete bulkhead that helps support the deck.

The deck structure itself houses a variety of storage areas. Trap doors lead to recessed boxes that hold hoses and sprinkler and fountain controls.

Design: Chaffee-Zumwalt & Associates.

RECEPTACLE below deck hides controls for sprinkling systems, fountains. Lid is removable.

WATER falls from cantilevered pool (at right) to second pool, then splashes to pool on ground.

SPACIOUS DECK on steeply sloping hillside provides space for children to play, adults to entertain and garden.

An angular deck fits contours of house

DECK *fits snugly into curve of house. Doors off bedroom (left), entry hall (center), living room (right) open onto patio. Floor-level deck steps down to small lower deck and terrace beyond.*

ANGLES *of wood decking make interesting design. Wrought iron railings are functional, decorative. Behind tree is bedroom door. Design: Herbert Frank, Victor W. Bowker.*

TREES *in deck slots provide shade. Across terrace is another deck for sunning and a view.*

Down the hillside—
from deck to deck to deck

Three decks provide outdoor living space at different elevations on a hillside lot. Separated by islands of landscaping, the decks blend into the surrounding forest. They required a minimum of site disturbance, so the structure runs little risk of washout; the bank's run-off is hardly altered. The decks were built around existing trees; none were removed.

Design: William G. Teufel.

LOWEST DECK has openings left for existing trees. Native conifers border its down-slope side.

MIDDLE DECK appears as island in midst of landscaping, native trees. Steps lead to first level.

HIGHEST of three decks is directly off house. Straight ahead are steps to middle level.

Three simple above-ground decks

DINING ROOM opens onto deck (left) large enough for outdoor dining, lounging. Design: Burr Richards. Living room is expanded by an upper deck (above) made of redwood 1 by 4's on 2 by 3-inch stringers. Design: Robert W. Hayes.

ANGLED DECK pushes out over slope and provides plenty of room for relaxing. Where deck is elevated most, railing boards are closer together for safety. Design: Chaffee-Zumwalt & Associates.

Deck ideas for special situations

WOODEN DECK is shaded by branches of large native oak. Slightly elevated, deck is separated from house by a garden of lichen-covered rocks bordered by shore juniper, mugho pine.

CONCRETE STEPPING PADS lead through gate to entry deck. Dining area, kitchen are adjoining inside rooms. Design: The Bumgardner Partnership.

TOWNHOUSE has deck off living room. Part is sheltered by glass window and by overhead. Stairs lead from the deck area down to a garden. Design: Bull, Field, Volkmann, Stockwell.

PAIR OF DECKS, separated by pools (left), replaced an unused slope. Each end has built-in seating. The two levels correspond to stepped heights of retaining wall. Design: Jack Chandler.

SIMPLE ELEVATED DECK backs up to rear fence, gives view of entire back garden. It is spacious enough for sunbathers, barbecue, and plants in containers. Design: Richard J. Kinsman.

MUMS add color to garden shelter. Design: Lincoln Fong.

The Separate Garden Room

There can be advantages to having a separate garden structure in addition to or instead of a patio adjoining the house. If such a shelter is planned carefully, it can become a second living room. A detached shelter can depart from the architectural style of the house, giving you more freedom in design and selection of materials. The shelter can be complex, or it can be simple enough for the homeowner to build. It could easily be constructed of 4 by 4-inch posts with a shed roof on top.

On hillside sites, or where the land's contours make a patio adjoining the house almost impossible, a separate structure may be the only way to get an outdoor living area into the garden. The freestanding garden structure also could be the solution for the homeowner whose house does not permit proper orientation of the patio. In a cool climate, a house whose patio exposure is on the cold north side presents a problem which might be solved by placing a shelter at the rear of the lot, facing the patio. The shelter becomes a south-facing

GIANT BAMBOO POLE supports roof of small, intimate garden room. Design: Bob Kutcher.

REDWOOD PAVILION is open structure with built-in seating on three sides. Decorative fixtures hold lights for nighttime illumination.

garden living room that traps the winter sun. In hot climates where the house faces into the summer sun, you can get the sun at your back by putting a shelter at the other side of the patio.

The shelter should be designed to serve the family's special interests and activities. It may be the form of a swimming pool bath house, or it can include greenhouse facilities for the gardener or special entertaining facilities. A separate shelter can provide children with a place to play away from the house during inclement weather.

If you are thinking of putting up an enclosed garden shelter, weigh its advantages against practical considerations. A close connection between the outdoor living room and the kitchen may be more advantageous than having the outdoor room independent of the house itself. Duplicating kitchen facilities can be very costly. When outdoor facilities are incomplete, a portable cart-like table can be used to transport food to and from the kitchen.

An important point to consider is the weather around your home. If the climate is pleasant the year around, you might want a fairly open structure; however, if the climate is cool, you will want to enclose the room and perhaps even insulate and heat it for year-round use.

Screened garden room for a cool retreat

A simple screened garden house, raised a few steps above a brick patio and an adjoining deck, provides a cool, insect-free retreat. It also functions as a garden divider, separating the pool from the outdoor sitting area off the living room. Its trellis roof extends out at one end to partly shade a dining table and benches for outdoor eating during good weather.

Design: Joseph Yamada.

SLIDING SCREENED DOORS on each side thwart insects. House, between pool and patio, is 12 by 12 feet inside; roof is 16 by 22 feet.

MULTIPURPOSE STRUCTURE is cool spot for serving refreshments on low table, a place to read, an extra outdoor room, a stage for flowering plants and bonsai. Cushions provide comfortable seating.

PALMS, FERNS thrive under roof constructed of 2 by 2's with fiberglass screening over the top.

Detached structures shade plants, people

LATHHOUSE has latticed sides, roof of 1 by 1's. Floor is concrete, as are steppingstones set in 2-inch river rock ground cover. Structure is shaded by walnut tree. Design: Warren Rienecker.

SIMPLE ALL-REDWOOD pavilion is 12 by 12 feet, stands at one end of a lawn terrace in a three-level garden. Back side is latticed for privacy; plants add color. Design: James Morrow.

TRIANGULARLY-ROOFED shelter is only shady place in sunny back yard. Paving is brick and concrete. Two triangular brick planters contain shade-loving plants. Design: Mrs. Neona Tott.

Gazebo is garden, outdoor living room

This latticed gazebo is decorated with a giant star and giant stripes, flags, and old-fashioned carnival lights. It forms the garden and outdoor social area for a long and narrow lot.

Redwood lattice encloses three sides and forms the roof. A fourth side and the wide entrance are open and face the swimming pool. The gazebo is predominantly white, with one blue wall to offset a giant white star, and angled red stripes on the other two walls. At night the carnival lights illuminate it inside or out.

Around and inside the gazebo is a terra cotta zoo of plant containers. There are 2½-foot-high lions, a chicken, a pig, and fish pots as well as some hanging containers.

Design: Gerald K. Lee.

GARDEN ROOM has brick floor, built-in bench. Lattice sides filter sun for plants and people.

Little gazebo for afternoon shade

Octagonal in shape, this gazebo sits on a small terrace overlooking garden and swimming pool. The shelter is only 11 feet in diameter, but it houses mechanical equipment for the pool and two dressing rooms besides forming a sun-protected outdoor room.

The gazebo has an open-beamed roof supported by eight 4½-inch diameter pipes sunk into the exposed aggregate flooring of the terrace. The walls and doors are ¾-inch exterior plywood; the fanciful top-knot is a vent for the pool heater. It is copper topped with a copper float of the type used in a toilet tank.

Design: Morgan Stedman.

PAVILION on upper terrace is shady place on warm afternoons.

Airy and open garden structures

REDWOOD GAZEBO (left) has wishbone-like lattice work—⅜-inch slats and spacer blocks are strung on ¼-inch metal rod (design: Germano Milono). Shelter (above) has open sides, half shingled roof, low benches (design: Marc Askew).

An outdoor room for a narrow side yard

NESTLED into narrow side yard is delightful shelter for summer dining. Structure was built around two tall redwoods which provide shade. Steppingstones, connecting house and shelter, were placed on gravel, give feeling of walking over stream.

Garden house is open to the breeze

SHELTER has A-peaked roof covered with canvas, brick floor. Fountain, pool are decorative and cool-looking elements. Firepit provides some heat, light. Additional illumination is from globe, floodlights under eaves. Design: Anthony Silvers.

Versatile and portable garden pavilions

Portable garden pavilions can liven up a garden or pool area. If you have several they can be treated as modular units or as separate little rooms. Three together can be placed over a long dining table, or they can be set singly in separate corners of the garden as serving pavilions for an outdoor buffet.

Each pavilion uses a 4 by 10-foot panel of 1/8-inch tempered hardboard. The frames—legs and top crosspieces—are finished 2 by 2's. White pine, redwood, cedar, and fir are all suitable woods. Fiberglass screening covers the top—it is weather resistant, and its open mesh gives shade but allows air circulation. Canvas, woven reed, or flat plastic panels will also work.

BAMBOO CURTAINS were added to pavilion as backdrop for serving table, make visual screen.

These leafy arbors are shaded retreats

CHINESE WISTERIA *cascades over arbor, a delightful place for outdoor dining. Pots of geraniums line arbor, add color. Design: Henry Sander, Jr.*

EASTER LILY VINE *grows along 1 by 3-inch lath, shades outdoor living-dining area. Bordering the planting bed is a built-in bench.*

ARBOR, *supported by pillars, has brick floor. Violet trumpet vine shades overhead; reed matting is stretched across beams for additional protection in summer.*

ATRIUM is central hall, provides access to all rooms of the house. Design: John L. Field.

Atriums and Lanais

Both the atrium and the lanai are part of the basic house structure. The atrium, located in the center of the house, is open to the sky but enclosed on four sides by the house walls. The lanai, on the other hand, is open on the sides and covered on top by the roof of the house.

The atrium is an idea that has been in use in some form since ancient times. On a small urban lot, it provides a private outdoor area completely shut off from the street and from the neighbors. On a large lot it can be the more intimate garden inside the house in contrast to the bigger, more open garden outside. In situations where most outdoor areas are windswept, the atrium offers shelter. And perhaps its most important contribution is that all the rooms of the house that face it have glass walls and share the light, air, and garden view.

Usually the atrium is room-sized, planned on an indoor rather than an outdoor scale. Plants should be scaled accordingly—select those that are slow-growing and neat; avoid plants that get sprawly or leggy.

LANAI adjoins dining room. Furniture, lantern, container plants, wall decorations, sink, counter transform simple space into useful and comfortable outdoor room. Design: Vladimir Ossipoff.

GLASS WALL faces private court, shaded by slats overhead. Atrium doubles width of living-dining rooms below, master bedroom above. Design: Killingsworth, Brady, Smith & Assocs.

An important point to remember is that the atrium is a potential sun trap. It may be fine in winter (in mild climates) but too hot in summer. To defend against too much direct sunlight, place plants and chairs in the shady places. Strategically placed sections of roof or overhead screen may be needed if the sun problem is serious. To improve air circulation, open a gate, door, or window that will draw cooler air into the atrium at a fairly low level. This will help warm air to rise more freely.

The lanai, an innovation from Hawaii, is an informal room incorporated into the basic design of the house. Protected by the roof of the house and glassed or walled in on one side, the lanai offers shade, rain and wind protection, air circulation, and a view of the garden.

In an area where the climate is not mild the year around, weather modifiers may have to be added to the lanai. It can be screened; a skylight roof can step up impact of the sun; a fireplace or radiant-heated floor can add warmth.

Although it is not impossible to add an atrium or a lanai to an existing structure, it might be more practical to consider these kinds of patios (especially the atrium) when building or remodeling your home.

The atrium opens to catch the breezes

TWO SECTIONS of house are separated by large atrium that is screened from the outside and open to the sky. Design: John Matthias.

SLIDING GLASS DOORS on one side of atrium open onto swimming pool. Bridge in split-level house connects sleeping quarters with living area.

BALCONIES off living room and master bedroom open wide to atrium for air circulation.

These houses have a hole in the center

HIGH GLASS WALLS at both ends give view straight through center of house. Roof arches over bedroom, living room; hole in center keeps house airy. Design: Claude Oakland & Assocs.

HOUSE, constructed on H plan, has two sections connected by loggia, separated by atrium walled off from street. High gable roof is for lofty views of sky, clouds, treetops. Design: Claude Oakland & Assocs.

Atriums make pleasant garden courtyards

GARDEN COURT is focal point of main living area. Entry, living room, dining room, and kitchen share its light and view. Design: Fish & Hodgkinson.

INTERIOR BRICK COURTYARD has screen overhead and around three sides at second floor level. Retracted awning pulls across under screen roof for shade. Design: John Matthias.

ORNAMENTAL fig which pokes through lath at top provides atrium with protection from the sun. Design: Lifescapes, Inc.

Two central courts with an airy feeling

ATRIUM (left), landscaped with pots of bamboo and palms, lets natural light inside. Design: Lakeview Homes. Central court (above) is divided in two by glass gallery linking entry, bedrooms. Design: Killingsworth, Brady, Smith & Associates.

Atrium connects two halves of house

This house is essentially in two parts with the living areas of the house on one side and the bedrooms on the other. In between and connecting the two halves is a 40-foot garden court with glass walls.

The atrium is sheltered from wind on all sides, yet is open to the sky. The use of obscure glass on two sides establishes privacy. Paving is stone.

Along each side of the court is a roofed walkway for use during inclement weather.

Design: Robin Boyd.

TEMPERATE and tropical plantings decorate atrium. Main part of house looks out at courtyard.

Lanais bring inside, outside together

Two lanais, one off the living-dining areas and one off the kitchen, expand the house out-of-doors. Every room has a view, and nearly every room has a sliding glass wall. Living space is almost independent of the wall line.

The long axis of the house parallels the prevailing winds. Thus, with the end closed, the sides can be opened without inviting a blast of wind through the interior.

Sheltering roof overhangs extend wide and low to cut out the glare of the sky and to keep rain far beyond open doors or windows. When it storms, all house walls can be closed.

Design: Vladimir Ossipoff.

KITCHEN LANAI is pleasant for informal dining. Outside, inside surfacing are same.

CONTINUOUS FLOOR and ceiling of living-dining rooms, lanai unify space subdivided by verticals. Draperies conceal stack of sliding glass doors.

LIVING ROOM expands out-of-doors into comfortable lanai— paved, planted, and roofed.

A screened lanai
doubled the living space

AIRY LANAI forms L around house, is spacious place for eating, sleeping, relaxing. Screening room keeps insects out but allows air circulation on four sides. Overhead provides protection from sun and rain. Design: Emrich Nicholson.

Lanai has kitchen,
storage facilities

ROOF of house extends over lanai which has sink, counter, storage facilities for furniture and games. Family room and lanai can be separated by sliding glass wall. Design: Edward Sullam.

LATH structure shades patio from sun. Design: Warren Lauesen.

Climate Controls for the Patio

There are many ways to modify the climate on a patio that receives too much sun or wind. Roofs and trees protect patios from the sun, while fencing or glass control the wind. Before you decide on what structure is right for your situation, consider the design of the patio, the house, and the garden. The weather modifier should be harmonious with the the surroundings.

A variety of overheads are available for sun control. They include egg-crate, lattice, screen, canvas, fiberglass, plastic, or aluminum. The overhead can be permanent, adjustable, or portable. Some roofs are solid, others transparent. A transparent roof offers protection but lets the light in.

Wind can be handled in two ways—it can either be diverted (turned aside to miss the protected area) or baffled (forced to pass through a screen). Trees, hedges, and fencing will do both; however, it takes several years for trees and hedges to be effective. Fences provide immediate protection. Glass and clear plastic wind screens work well if you want to block the wind but not the view.

UPPER DECK is perfect on pleasant day. If sun is too hot, the place to be is on ground-level patio shaded by deck above. Design: Calvin Straub.

RAISED BENCHLIKE platform, sitting area of brick patio, is shaded by spreading branches of mature apricot tree. Design: Jean Davidson.

GARDEN HOUSE, connected to dining room by glassed-in hall, is ideal for year-round entertaining. Warmth comes from heat register, sun coming through plastic ceiling, glass walls. Temperature inside is easily controlled by opening any or all of nine pairs of double doors. Design: Keith Kolb & Assocs.

Egg-crate grids
for shade and shadows

You can get a small degree of sun conditioning with an egg-crate overhead. It provides slight shade, protection from slanting direct sun rays in morning or late afternoon, and even a little wind deflection.

The grids do not interfere with the free flow of air. They do create strong shadow patterns on the patio as the sun moves across the sky.

GENEROUS OVERHEAD (above) is egg-crate style. Translucent center section shades aggregate patio but allows light to filter through. At right, 1 by 4's in egg-crate make interesting design.

This trellis serves
a double purpose

SUNNING BENCH is shaded by trellis designed to give overhead protection with minimum obstruction from vertical supports. Trellis, block wall separate pool from garden. Design: Jones & Peterson.

Laths filter sun's rays, wind's force

Lath or lattice structures, wood strips spaced apart and supported by beams and crosspieces, filter the direct rays of the sun. (The degree of filtration depends on how close together you put the strips.) They also break the force of the wind without stopping vertical air circulation. Climbing vines can be trained on lath overheads to increase sun control.

The lattice roofs shown here are more elaborate than usual. They are freestanding and not attached directly to the house.

SLATS in slanting planes of entry overhead produce changing pattern of filtered sun and full shade on pavement. Design: John Matthias.

ENTRY GARDEN is shaded by two freestanding latticed overheads which are supported by slender steel posts. Upper sunshade is 12 feet high at point of V, rises to 15 feet over eave at right.

BACK GARDEN is shaded by double slanting planes that rise from 10-foot height at right to 14 feet over eave at left.

Two canvas awnings for climate protection

Good quality canvas, properly installed, will shade the patio from sun, withstand strong winds, and shed rain water. Its tightly woven texture does retard air movement.

As canvas is a fairly light material, it requires less support and framing than is necessary for a wood overhead. However, since the canvas functions as a sail, the support for the overhead must be very sturdy and firmly anchored.

Canvas comes painted with acrylics or vinyl for color and for protection. Some synthetic substitutes suitable for awnings are acrylic fiber, woven fiberglass, or vinyl-coated nylon.

FOUR-STRIP canvas awnings can be pulled to shade patio. Springs on hooks (above) maintain tension against canvas stretch, wind flapping. Wooden bars make canvas fold, stack neatly. Design: Royston, Hanamoto, Mayes & Beck.

CANVAS SHADE woven over and under two levels of pipe is kept taut, doesn't flap in wind or sag over 16-foot span. A-shaped design allows air circulation. Design: Royston, Hanamoto, Mayes & Beck.

Fiberglass—a
weatherproof patio roof

FIBERGLASS OVERHEAD protects patio from sun and rain but lets light filter through. It is light-weight, easy to put in place, and requires little or no maintenance. Design: Lawrence Underhill.

Overheads made
from natural materials

SPLIT BAMBOO shades patio. Roll-up blinds are spread out over wood frame and tacked down (right). Design: Burr Garman. Patio and pool above are shaded by strips of ocotillo. Design: Cliff May.

Screens give year-round climate control

Aluminum or fiberglass screening not only protects against the hot sun but also against insects and windborne litter.

Screened panels on the sides and top will keep the area open to maximum light and air. During the warm months, substitute panels that afford some shade could be placed across the top. If afternoon sun is a problem, use roll-down blinds of fiberglass woven to reflect the sun and reduce glare without blocking the view entirely or interfering too much with air circulation. If more protection is required, substitute panels of some translucent material on the weather sides.

Fiberglass screening is available in many colors; however, darker colors have better see-through quality. There's little or no light reflection, so views out and in are sharper. Lighter colors reflect light, so visibility in and out is reduced. They do offer a degree of privacy, reflect heat better, and keep the enclosure cooler.

Aluminum louvered screens block out the sun while still allowing air circulation. The space between louvers is small enough to keep out most insects. Visibility out is somewhat reduced, but people outside cannot see in. The material can be used in wood or metal frames.

METAL-FRAMED fiberglass screens patio entered from house or through two sliding doors. Leaves hose off top. Design: Michael Painter.

SIDE PANELS of aluminum screening, top panels of translucent plastic fasten onto permanent wood structure for climate control. Design: G. E. Talbot.

LOUVERED aluminum screening on sides and top of deck blocks sun but not view. Air circulates between panels and through screening. Design: Jon F. Myhre.

These patio overheads are adjustable

SMALL PATIO has choice of sun or shade. Overhead panels of split bamboo slide along tracks in wood frame. Bamboo pole is used for adjusting the panels. Design: Allen J. Johannesen.

ADJUSTABLE LOUVERS are operated like giant horizontal Venetian blind. Metal arm runs along 1 by 6 louvers, is attached to cable which operates louvers from below. Design: Weston Smith.

SUN SHELTER has top angled toward afternoon sun. Roof has three 4 by 8-foot panels of louvers independently operated by rod underneath. Slats are 1 by 6's, pivot at ends on aluminum pins. Design: Albert Stadtegger.

Three freestanding sun roofs

Freestanding shelters have certain advantages. They can be less expensive to construct than those attached to the house. It is not as important that they be harmonious with the house style and its structural materials. Size does not have to be in proportion to that of the house. And all four walls can be open to circulating air.

UMBRELLA STAND has 2-foot circular base of ¼-inch plywood edged with corrugated steel. Electrical conduit (sleeve for pole) is centered in stand, anchored with hand-mixed concrete.

WOOD-AND-REED UMBRELLA made of 2 by 8-inch frame sits on column of four 4 by 4's, shades patio from midday sun. Design: Burr Garman.

GIANT CANVAS parasol, 9½ feet across, is held to fence by metal brackets, casts large circle of shade. Design: Royston, Hana-moto, Mayes & Beck.

Trees and vines
for natural shade

Trees can be effective in shading sun-filled patios. They are available in all stages of growth; however, it will take a young tree several years before it supplies adequate shade.

Globe-shaped or umbrellalike trees (ash, elm) cast shade directly below but give little protection from the slanting rays of the sun. Tall, pyramid-shaped trees (cypress, poplar, eucalyptus) if planted close together in a screen protect from the glare of the late sun but provide scant shade when the sun is overhead. Shade trees with low-lying branches cut sunlight away from their bases and affect your plantings; trees with fanning branches allow light to reach ground-level plants.

Vines can be trained along an overhead or upwards on walls or supports. A deciduous vine will shade the patio in summer but allow sunlight to get through in winter. Evergreen vines will shade the year around. Vines add color during their blooming season—spring or summer.

Vines have some shortcomings. Many varieties require persistent pruning. Rampant vines can cause a patio to look neglected. Also, some kinds attract bees.

SPREADING BRANCHES of mature apple tree shade octagonal decked seating area around its base and a portion of the concrete patio.

GROVE of wide-spreading mesquite trees shelters brick patio and a planting of cactus and succulents from desert sun. Design: Herbert J. Bool.

JAPANESE WISTERIA on rafter-like support shades patio, makes interesting shadow patterns, adds sprays of color in spring.

Garden houses with sun, wind protection

TRELLISLIKE overhead of 2 by 2's filters shade. Back section has plastic panels for rain protection. Two sides are sheltered from wind by panels of hardboard and removable windows. Frames are secured by turn buttons. Design: William Kapranos.

WIND is controlled by panels of clear glass and tempered hardboard on two sides. Open space above and below panels allows for air circulation. Flat overhead provides shade. Design: N. Bob Murakami.

Glass doors, trellis shelter deck

OVERHEAD TRELLIS is 3 by 3's covered with corrugated white, translucent fiberglass reinforced panels, protects deck from sun, rain, dew.

SLIDING DOORS of tempered glass stop wind on exposed end of deck without blocking view. They're a regular three-door, three-track commercial unit; each 6-foot-wide door slides independently.

SPACIOUS DECK, sheltered from the sun and the wind, is pleasant outdoor sitting and dining area. Design: Kahl & Lowry.

Glass wall stops wind, canvas roof stops sun

This terrace is well-protected from the wind and sun but is open to the view. Trees were planted on the hillside to filter the sun and wind but were trimmed to preserve the view. A glass wall shields the section of terrace along the living and dining rooms. The canvas overhead shades the terrace and blocks wind currents that might swirl over the glass wall. It is supported and stiffened against flapping by awning poles that stretch from the eave to the glass wall.

The north end of the terrace was left open, exposing one section of the patio to full sun. It, too, is sheltered from the wind—by ordinary fencing on two sides and the louvered doors and some glass on the third.

Design: Joseph Copp, Jr.

GLASS WALLS keep terrace calm even on breezy days. Canvas roof keeps sun, wind out.

CANVAS ROOF is lashed to eyebolts in wood frame. Spaces allow warm air to flow up and out.

FOLDING louvered doors separate enclosed area from outdoor terrace. Brick surface inside is continued out-of-doors.

Pivoting fiberglass screens direct wind

This open-and-shut screen keeps the wind out or lets the wind in. The screen has stationary panels of bamboo poles alternated with movable panels of translucent fiberglass. The movable panels can also control sunlight. When they're shut, the fiberglass lets light through but reduces sun glare.

Each panel in the screen is 25 by 68 inches, enclosed with a frame of 2 by 2½-inch wood strips. The bamboo poles were shaped at the ends to slip into ½ by ½-inch grooves at the top and bottom of each frame; the frames are nailed to a supporting structure of 2 by 6's. The fiberglass panels fit into ⅛ by ½-inch grooves in the sides, top, and bottom of their frames.

The fiberglass panels can pivot 180 degrees. Open one panel a certain degree and all others on the same edge of the deck open equally because all are connected by a long rod at the back of the screen. The rod is attached to a 2 by 6-inch metal plate screwed to the top of each wood frame.

Each panel pivots on ⅜-inch bolts (with two washers) set at the center of the top and bottom of the frame; the bolts ride in holes drilled in the 2 by 6's that form the supporting structure.

Design: Charles F. Martin.

FIBERGLASS PANELS pivot easily to let breezes cross deck. Bamboo panels are stationary.

These are swinging glass wind screens

Pivoting clear glass panels protect the patio from the wind without blocking the view. The 4 by 5-foot panels are held in place top and bottom by metal pins inserted at midpoint through each screen frame and into the window frame. A metal plate with a notch in it, attached to the framework, swings around to lock each pin. The window sashes can thus swivel in place to control the breezes. When closed, vertical slide bolts in the left corners hold them tight. The pins are easy to remove, and the sashes lift out for winter storage.

Design: Alan Liddle.

LARGE glass panels swing on steel pins, protect patio from wind without hindering view.

These panels pivot on nails

These pivoting patio screens can be adjusted to whatever angle you need to control the breezes. They are also good for sun control or privacy.

Their framing is simply 2 by 2's. Flat white fiberglass panels (36 inches wide) are stapled over the frames, and a ⅜ by 1¾-inch trim is tacked over the staples. Each screen pivots at top on a ⅜-inch lag screw with washer, screwed into a wood beam above through a hole in the middle of the top 2 by 2. The bottoms pivot on 20-penny nails (they carry no weight) through the middle of the lower 2 by 2's and into ¾-inch-deep holes in the floor.

Design: Gregory Mull.

LIGHTWEIGHT *fiberglass screen is held open by a single pin dropped into small hole in brick floor.*

SMALL PINS *at door-handle height hold panels closed. The closed screens admit light.*

PINS *are simply galvanized 20-penny nails with their points cut off. Upper screwbolt holds the pin when it is not needed.*

Three ideas
for weather protection

DECK has fiberglass side and roof panels set between Douglas fir posts. Plastic windows have a stained-glass design. Design: Placido R. Perez.

LARGE PANELS of tempered glass in redwood framework of 2 by 4's form protective windbreak. Two sections of screen slide open on heavy-duty hardware. Simple locking device—large bent nail on chain that slips into hole in frame—is at top. Glass wall also creates sun pocket and keeps children out of pool area. Design: Harold Bakke.

CURVED PERGOLA has latticed roof, is wind baffle for exposed aggregate patio. Built-in redwood seating cantilevers from frame. Design: Katy & Paul Steinmetz.

FLAGSTONES are bordered by sweet alyssum, dichondra.

Surfacing Materials for the Patio

There are many excellent patio surfacing materials to choose from. Brick, tile, concrete, flagstone, wood, or adobe blocks are all fine durable materials—if used in the right place and competently installed. Each of these materials has advantages and disadvantages; when selecting the material for your patio, keep the following points in mind.

A pavement should have a pleasing surface texture: one that doesn't glare; one that is non-skid. A soft-appearing texture is more appealing than one that looks hard and slick.

Patio paving should be reasonably easy to take care of. Stains from food or mud should be removable without drastic action. The paving shouldn't require frequent overhauling.

The surface should level off smoothly for swift drainage and for easy movement of furniture and people.

The material should harmonize with the construction materials used in the

FOOT-SQUARE concrete pads alternated with Irish moss give patio checkerboard surface. Greenery softens feeling of concrete. Design: Thomas Batty.

PATIO PAVEMENT is handcrafted tiles, beach and river pebbles, flagstone, scored concrete. Design: Eckbo, Dean, Austin & Williams.

house and garden structure (if any). It should also harmonize with the textures and tones of the garden plantings.

The surfacing material should be one that can be put in place at a reasonable cost to you.

Paving should be weather-resistant. It shouldn't sag, buckle, or crack in cold weather or get so warm underfoot that it is uncomfortable to walk on. If you want to store the day's heat, you need one kind of paving; if you wish to dispel it, you should choose another.

If you want to put the surfacing down yourself, you will want to know if this is possible. Some types are easily put in place, others call for heavy machinery. Give your patio floor a good foundation—this will greatly affect the life span of your paving.

There are several materials that can be used to supplement existing paving or for temporary surfacing. They are generally inexpensive and easy to apply. Wood chips, by-products of mills, are springy, soft, and easily scattered. To work successfully as a patio surface, they should be confined in a grid system of headers. Other materials are gravel or crushed rocks which work best as a topping over bedrock or decomposed granite.

Brick paving is handsome in any situation

Bricks provide a handsome, non-glare surface that blends with almost any structural material and looks at ease in a garden. Bricks are available in different textures, from rough to almost tile-smooth. Of the two kinds of bricks, common and face, common bricks are most used by home craftsmen and are less expensive than face. Exact dimensions of a standard brick vary from region to region and manufacturer to manufacturer. Traditionally, the color of brick has been the color of clay—a red or red-brown. However, now clay bricks come in tones of ebony, buff, fawn, and red. Brick prices vary—from 6 to 20 cents or more per brick.

Before paving with bricks, be sure the water drains away from the area. Shifting and problems with efflorescence (white deposits) can result if water stands under the bricks.

Bricks are relatively easy to put down; however, some bonds, or patterns, can demand a good bit of accuracy and brick cutting. Bricks can be set in sand or mortar. Unless you live where the ground freezes, bricks set in sand are as permanent and durable as bricks set in mortar. If you want a rustic, antique look to your paving, use dry mortar. For a clean, tooled, or shaped mortar joint between bricks, use wet mortar.

BUFF BRICKS, set in jack-on-jack pattern, keep enclosed dining patio bright. This bond requires some accuracy, possibly no cutting.

TERRACED GARDEN has brick surface in diagonal herringbone pattern. This is one of the more difficult patterns; lots of cutting is necessary.

USING WIDE JOINTS in dry mortar gives worn look, is good with broken or uneven bricks.

A concrete floor can be plain or fancy

Concrete paving offers permanence, wearability, and low cost, especially if you do it yourself. However, putting down concrete is hard work, and if you have any doubts about doing the job yourself, it might be wise to call on a contractor.

Concrete can be natural or colored, smooth or textured. Disadvantages to leaving the concrete plain are a harsh surface, glare, and a commercial feeling. To break up the expanse of concrete, separate the area into small squares divided by header boards or bricks. The squares of concrete can be mixed with blocks of grass. For a more sophisticated finish, you can have concrete smoothed lightly or heavily brushed, washed to expose the aggregate, seeded with rock salt for a pocked effect, surfaced with handsome pebbles, swirled, scored, or patterned. If you pave with pebbles, press them in after the concrete is poured. How far you press them determines the smoothness of the finish.

ELABORATE FLOOR has hand-placed colored stones in alternate stripes. Each stripe was formed, poured separately. Design: Ted Bower.

HARD RUBBER FLOAT gives concrete pads sand finish without lines or swirls. Spaces between pads were filled with concrete, hosed and brushed for exposed aggregate finish. Design: Robert Chittock.

PAVING blocks form patio's surface, shaded by Japanese pagoda trees. Design: S. A. Sanfilippo.

Flagstones—expensive but very durable

Flagstones are the most expensive of surfacing materials, but they give unmatched permanence if properly laid. Their soft colors (buff, yellow, brownish red, gray) bring warmth to the patio, while their irregular shapes and sculptured surface add pattern and texture to the garden floor. However, to some people, flagstones look cold and quarry-like; their colors and random patterns are hard to work into subdued results. As a compromise, imitation flagstone can be cast in concrete with pleasing results.

There are different types of stones available from building material dealers. They come in either irregular or rectangular shapes. The simplest way to lay flagstones is by placing them directly on the soil. For more stability, lay the flagstones in sand. For the most permanency, set the stones on a 3-inch slab of concrete and bed them in mortar.

IRREGULAR FLAGSTONES set in small mortar joints give fairly even surface, harmonize with structural materials of the house and pond.

Tile can give a rough or smooth look

Tiles give a smooth look to a patio. They are easy to clean, resist stains and scratches, and withstand heavy foot traffic. Tiles are expensive and so is the installation. However, the cost can be kept down by using tile in conjunction with bricks or concrete.

Although tile comes in several sizes, colors, and shapes, it usually belongs to one of two groups—quarry tile or patio tile. Both are manufactured products. Quarry tile is the most expensive to manufacture and is the most regular in shape. Patio tile is available in rough, handcrafted shapes. Tiles can be set in sand, in mortar, or over concrete.

WHITE mortar joints, smooth tiles in straightforward pattern give patio clean and formal look.

Adobe bricks for an early Spanish feeling

Adobe blocks, with their warm and friendly air, look particularly comfortable in the patio of a ranch-style home. Easy to install, the blocks are laid in a sand bed in about the same way as clay bricks. They contain an asphaltic stabilizer which keeps them from dissolving in the winter and cracking in the summer. Limitations of adobe blocks are that they tend to crumble at the edges, that they wear away gradually, and that they store up heat, restricting their value to cooler patios.

SAND JOINTS around adobe blocks can be planted with ground cover for softening effect.

Wood brings a natural look to the garden

Wood paving with its warm color and soft texture brings a touch of the forest into your garden. There are several ways of using wood—round discs can be put down on sand in random fashion; square blocks can be set like bricks in a standard paving pattern; or strips of lumber can be used for a deck.

Redwood rounds or blocks will eventually have to be replaced. The end grain is in constant contact with ground moisture that seeps up through the sand bed. The open grain soaks up the water, causing bacterial and insect growth. The wood then either rots away or succumbs to insects. Treating the wood with a preservative before installation helps. Blocks and rounds are also sensitive to the weather. Best in shady spots, they crack and warp in sunny locations; they will also freeze and split in heavy frosts.

PATIO FLOOR surfaced with redwood rounds is in keeping with wooded site, rustic house.

SEATING, lights, overhead, serving counter make patio complete.

Making the Patio Livable

Once you have decided on the structural elements of the patio, you can turn to the finishing touches. There are several features, both functional and decorative, that you might wish to incorporate into your outdoor room.

If your patio needs privacy from neighboring houses, you can put up fences, walls, or screens. Landscaping is also effective.

Container plants, hanging pots, or border plantings can soften the hard mechanical lines of a fence, bench, or wall, brighten the patio with blossoms, and freshen the air with their fragrance. Container plants can be placed on steps or in a corner, clustered around porch posts or tree trunks, or lined up against the house. Large shrubs or small trees do well in big containers. They can be used to divert traffic through the patio. Their leaf patterns create interesting designs.

A garden pool or fountain brings the sight and sound of water into the garden. A reflecting pool should be situated out of the wind so the surface is quiet.

BUILT-IN SEATING *around perimeter of deck is good for lounging. Low table of oak wood makes elegant setting for bonsai. Design: Joseph Yamada.*

FOUNTAIN, *surrounded by tree chrysanthemums, is focal point of patio. Vines, ferns add intimate feeling. Design: C. Jacques Hahn.*

Good lighting is both functional and aesthetic. You want certain areas of your patio to be well-lighted, such as around the swimming pool. But you can also use lights for special effects—to highlight a shrub, tree, vine, or piece of garden sculpture. For high-intensity illumination, floodlights or spotlights are most satisfactory. Lamps come in various styles and sizes. Low-voltage wiring is available, and once past the transformer, it is safe for the homeowner to install.

You can extend the usability of your patio by adding some form of heating. There are gas-fed infrared heaters, both portable and permanent. Firepits (which can also double as a barbecue) and braziers are also good sources of heat. You could even construct an outdoor fireplace. Probably the most satisfactory (but most expensive) way to warm the patio is to have a radiant heating system installed in or under the patio floor.

If you like to dine outdoors, you might want to incorporate a built-in barbecue into the patio design. It can be inconspicuous, constructed as part of the chimney, or it can be a separate unit. If separate, keep the barbecue in scale—be sure the unit is not so large as to overwhelm the patio.

You will want to have places to sit on the patio. Built-in seating (benches and bench walls) can be designed to handle most entertaining situations. You will also want movable chairs and tables that can be positioned to fit the situation.

This screen drops down for privacy

BASSWOOD SHADE hangs on high extension of railing at one end of deck, pulls up or rolls down, also stops at any point. Design: Burr Richards.

Zigzag fence hides patio from the street

ENTRY PATIO is fenced with vertical 1 by 2-inch laths spaced ½ inch apart for the upper 4½ feet, horizontal siding for the lower 2½ feet. Laths appear solid from street. Design: Robert Fleckenstein.

Three ideas
for patio privacy

SCREEN with stained glass insets blocks view of utility yard from patio and forms one wall of airy ramada. Design: Charles Clement.

ROUNDED WALL conceals patio from driveway. Grille posts allow light to filter through to sitting area and to plants. Design: Armstrong & Sharfman.

EIGHT-FOOT-LONG screen separates patio off bedroom from main outdoor area, has flat plastic panels and 1 by 2's in frame of 2 by 4's. Design: Robert Babcock.

This yard was landscaped for privacy

Landscaping here solved the privacy problem of living at the bottom of a hill and the problem of a stark 12-foot-high retaining wall on two sides of the patio. The solution included a 6-foot asbestos-cement privacy fence atop the wall, a freestanding pergola with plastic arches to block the view, and a rock garden planted with handsome ferns to disguise the blank wall.

Design: John Hans Ostwald.

PLASTIC ARCHES on top pergola contribute to privacy from house above. Waterfall cascades down from 6-foot fence to floor-level pool.

PERGOLA of trellis and plastic "vaults" is visual barrier, provides partial shade for new rock and fern garden that masks high retaining wall.

PATIO has complete privacy. Plantings help lessen the impression of great height.

Hanging plants add color to the patio

TRAILING SPIDER plant (left) in ceramic container hangs from tree, adds greenery to patio. Above, round pots, threaded on long metal rods which hang from ceiling joists, are planted with combination of begonias, coleus, Hahn's ivy.

FUCHSIAS AND BEGONIAS in wire baskets hang from patio roof, add seasonal color to patio. Overhead is ribbed fiberglass on top of a lath structure. Wisteria will eventually cover the overhead.

Patio landscaping using border plantings

CLEAR YELLOW TULIPS growing tall against high whitewashed brick privacy wall brighten small entry patio. Design: Bain & Overturf.

VERTICAL BANDS of xylosma soften wall and reduce glare in sunny patio. Blooming bulbs, annuals at base of vine add color. Design: Guy Greene.

LOW WALL bordering adobe brick patio holds masses of bright and colorful marigolds, zinnias. Design: Mrs. James A. Hinze.

Container plants
for movable color

FLATS of dwarf marigolds, sweet alyssum, pansies, verbenas slipped into simple white wooden collars give instant color to the patio.

CEDAR PLANKS, sandblasted and weathered to a soft gray, make a good bench for displaying container plants outdoors. Design: Esta James.

POTS of geraniums give patio a brilliant display of color, can be moved for weather protection.

Fountains, waterfalls add sound of splashing water

LIGHTWEIGHT rock is carved with hammer or chisel to create waterway. Water can be diverted for a foaming, churning, or cascading effect.

WATER LILIES stand above pond water, were placed out of range of fountain splash to prevent damage to blossoms. Design: Houghton Sawyer.

FOUNTAIN is set among Tasmanian tree ferns, has a concrete base and a thick-pebbled bowl.

Garden pools are decorative elements

STONE FIGURE OF JIZO (above), Japanese guardian of children, sits in pool hollowed out of 1½ by 2-foot granite block. Design: Takano Nakamura. Small 3 by 5-foot pool (left) with decorative tile trim holds white star water lilies.

REFLECTING POOL, bordered by decked sitting area, has concrete steppingstones across it, a flat-pebbled bottom. Douglas fir casts shadows across pool area. Design: Chaffee-Zumwalt & Assocs.

Three ways to light the patio

METAL LAMP lights plants bordering patio. Top has hole for easy bulb changing, is galvanized for rust prevention. Design: Carol Wieting.

TUBELIKE LIGHT, concealed by panel of translucent plastic is 6½ feet high, 16 inches wide. Effect is soft, glare-free glow. Design: Jerry Gropp.

HANGING PLANTER can also be light fixture. Cool 12-volt lights do not affect delicate plants, such as ferns. Note installation through container's drain hole.

Heating units increase patio usability

GAS-FIRED infrared heater radiates heat without visible flame, is unaffected by a breeze, is mounted to direct heat downward. Cord has control switch.

PORTABLE gas-fired infrared patio heater casts 12 to 15-foot circle of radiant heat.

FIREPIT is 14 inches deep, has firebrick sides, sand floor. Two quarry tile lids cover firepit when not in use. Design: Warren Lauesen.

Three ideas for patio cooking, serving

BARBECUE, incorporated into flagstone wall, is ideal for small patio. Smoke from cooking is released through chimney. Design: Jack Finnegan.

GRILL, attached to wall outside kitchen, has slate-covered counter. Hood carries smoke up through roof. Design: Armstrong & Sharfman.

WIDE SHELF outside kitchen counter and generous opening is for passing food out to deck.

Built-in and movable patio furniture

READY-MADE chairs, table can be moved for use in sun or shade. Pattern blends with surroundings.

WOODEN BENCH, back rest are built in as part of fence. Trellis overhead partially shades sitting area. Design: Glen Hunt & Associates.

VERSATILE BENCH can be garden seat, table, sun deck, or work center. Design: Joseph McGie.

PHOTOGRAPHERS

WILLIAM APLIN: 13 left; 15 left; 22 top left, right; 23 top left; 28 bottom; 38 bottom right; 40 top left; 83 top right, bottom right; 91 right, top left; 94 top left; 101 left; 115 left; 116 bottom; 119 top right; 121 top right. ARCHITECTURAL PHOTOGRAPHERS: 113 bottom. MORLEY BAER: 66 bottom right; 74 bottom left; 81 top left; 84; 123 bottom. JERRY BRAGSTAD: 18; 57 bottom right. ERNEST BRAUN: 7 left; 14; 15 right; 24 top left; 28 top right; 32; 33 top left; 35; 55 top right, bottom; 73 top right; 74 top left; 87; 88 top right, left; 90; 97 bottom left; 102 top left, top right; 122 bottom left; 123 top right; 126 left; 127 top left. ARTHUR BRAVO: 107 top left. TOM BURNS, JR.: 82 left, top right. CALIFORNIA REDWOOD ASSOCIATION: 55 top left; 77 left. CLYDE CHILDRESS: 120 top left. GLENN CHRISTIANSEN: 6 right; 10 bottom left; 29; 33 top right; 38 left, top right; 39; 43; 46 bottom left; 60; 78; 80 bottom right; 82 bottom right; 83 left; 89 top left; 93 bottom; 103; 109 left; 115 right; 121 left; 123 top left; 125 bottom right. BETTY CLINTON: 71; 126 top right. ROBERT COX: 105 top. LYN DAVIS: 101 bottom right. RICHARD DAWSON: 5 left; 46 right, top left. MAX ECKERT: 51 top right; 117 left. DWAIN FAUBION: 65 bottom left, right. FEATHEROCK, INC.: 122 top left. RICHARD FISH: 7 right; 9 left, bottom right; 11 left, bottom right; 19 top right, bottom; 24 bottom left; 25 top right, bottom right; 27; 30 bottom left, right; 31 bottom; 34; 37 bottom; 40 top right, bottom; 44; 47; 49; 50 top left, top right; 53 top right; 56; 58 top left, top right; 59; 61; 62; 66 left, top right; 72; 75 top left, top right; 77 right; 88 bottom right; 92; 94 top right, bottom; 95; 98 top left, bottom left; 104; 114. JOSHUA FREIWALD: 25 left; 53 bottom. FRANK L. GAYNOR: 17 top left, right; 42; 50 bottom; 51 bottom right; 117 top right. R. E. GULBRANSON: 125 top right. JOHN HARTLEY: 22 bottom. ART HUPY: 28 top left; 65 top; 81 bottom left. FRANK JENSEN: 16. NEIL KOPPES: 31 top left, right; 93 top right. ROY KRELL: 24 right; 97 top, bottom right; 100 right. EDMUND Y. LEE: 54. ELLS MARUGG: 12 right; 13 right; 41 bottom; 58 bottom; 107 right; 111 bottom right; 120 bottom left; 122 right; 127 bottom left. MASTER POOLS BY FIESTA POOLS: 52 top left. GLENN MITCHELL: 9 top right. KEN MOLINO: 107 bottom left. DON NORMARK: 4; 11 top right; 12 left; 17 bottom left; 19 top left; 21; 23 right, bottom left; 33 bottom; 36 bottom left, right; 37 top left, right; 41 top left, right; 48; 57 left, top right; 63; 64 top left; 67; 68; 70; 73 top left, bottom; 74 right; 75 bottom; 99 left; 105 bottom; 108; 109 right; 111 left, top right; 116 top left, top right; 119 top left, bottom; 120 right; 121 bottom right; 124 right, top left; 127 right. KURT E. OSTWALD: 118. PHIL PALMER: 96; 100 bottom left. MAYNARD PARKER: 112 top. POOLS BY RAPP: 52 bottom left. PETE REDPATH: 125 left. KARL RIEK: 45 left; 64 top right. MARTHA ROSMAN: 93 top left; 98 right; 106. WILLIAM SEARS: 36 top left. JULIUS SHULMAN: 85 left; 89 right. DOUGLAS SIMMONDS: 52 right. HUGH H. STRATFORD: 20 top left, right; 64 bottom; 69. MARK STRIZEC: 89 bottom left. DARROW WATT: 5 right; 6 left; 8; 10 top left; 20 bottom; 30 top left; 45 right; 51 left; 53 top left; 76; 79 left, top right; 80 top left; 81 right; 86; 99 top right, bottom right; 100 top left; 101 top right; 102 bottom; 110; 117 bottom right; 124 bottom left; 126 bottom right. R. WENKAM: 85 right; 91 bottom left. MASON WEYMOUTH: 113 top. JOE WILLIAMSON: 79 bottom right. DOUG WILSON: 26. GEORGE WOO: 10 right.